EXTRATERRESTRIALS

First published in 1998 by Macdonald Young
Books, an imprint of Wayland Publishers
Limited, 61 Western Road, Hove, East
Sussex, BN3 1JD

© Macdonald Young Books 1998

Look for Macdonald Young Books on the
Internet at: http://www.myb.co.uk

Commissioning editor: Hazel Songhurst
Designer: Chris Leishman
Project Editors: Hazel Songhurst and Lisa
Edwards
Illustrator: Colin Sullivan
Consultant: Philip Mantle, Former Director
of Investigation for British UFO Research
Association

Picture acknowledgments:
Camera Press 21 (Martin Argles), Fortean
Picture Library 7(l),17(c)(br), Images 15(t),
25(t), 27(l), 28(tl), (The Charles Walker
Collection), John Frost 13, 14, Robert Harding
11, 27(b), Mary Evans Picture Library 9(br),
17(t), 27(t), Getty Images 9(t) (Steven Peters),
23(tr) (James Balog), 28(bl) (Art Wolfe),
Topham Picturepoint 25(l)

A CIP catalogue record for this book is
available from the British Library

ISBN 0 7500 2530 1

576.839
001-942

Printed and bound in Belgium by Proost N.V.

Ivor Baddiel was a primary school teacher
before becoming a full-time writer and
broadcaster.
Tracey Blezard is an English language
teacher and a writer specializing in
teenage fiction.

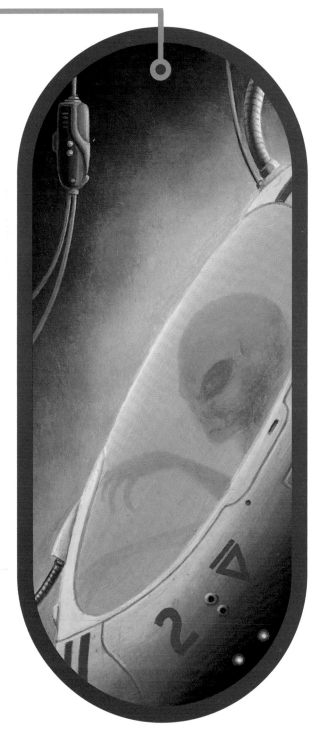

MYSTERIOUS WORLD

EXTRATERRESTRIALS

Investigations into the unexplained

Ivor Baddiel & Tracey Blezard

MACDONALD YOUNG BOOKS

Contents

About this Book

Our galaxy alone contains 100,000 million stars – of which scientists believe an astonishing 10,000 million have the conditions necessary to sustain life. Here on Earth, scientists and observers search the skies for vital signs that WE ARE NOT ALONE. No one has yet unravelled the mystery of whether or not extraterrestrial life exists. Can you?

In this book we provide the information you need to try and solve the puzzle of apparently inexplicable extraterrestrial encounters. For each mystery, study the evidence – based on real case-histories – and balance it against the latest popular theories. Consider the current scientific view, think about the questions that end each section – then come up with your answer.

Hundreds of thousands of reports of alien activity and encounters have been logged worldwide and yet definite proof has never been found. Could it be that, as astronomer Alan Lothian believes: "Absence of evidence is not evidence of absence"? Perhaps we are simply misreading the signals and ignoring the evidence that is plainly before us.

Remember. The truth may well be out there but you won't find it unless you are looking for it.

Strange Sightings

It is estimated that about every two minutes around the world, an Unidentified Flying Object (UFO) sighting is reported. Investigators are able to reclassify more than 90% of the sightings as Identified Flying Objects (IFOs), leaving just a small minority of cases where clear explanations prove difficult.

THE MYSTERY

When people see strange objects in the sky, could they really be alien craft from outer space or are people witnessing extraordinary natural phenomena that we do not yet fully understand?

THE EVIDENCE

During World War Two, American pilots over Europe reported glowing lights tailing their aircraft, which they named 'foo fighters' after a popular cartoon. The lights were among the first officially investigated UFOs and explanations for them included: aluminium foil released by planes to confuse enemy radar; a new type of weapon; and St. Elmo's Fire, a naturally occurring ball of static electricity. For the witnesses, however, these explanations failed to describe the silvery discs which chased their aircraft.

Two apparently genuine photographs of UFOs were taken in 1950 by a couple in Oregon, USA, who described the UFO as looking and behaving like a structured, powered disc. Scientists who examined the photographs finally classified them 'Unexplained'.

In 1952, an American CIA (Central Intelligence Agency) official was holding a garden party when a UFO appeared before his stunned guests, performed aerial manoeuvres and then disappeared. The incident was filed 'Unknown'.

Early one morning in 1954, Frenchman Bernard Miserey spotted a huge cigar-shaped object suspended over the River Seine. Five discs dropped from it and sped off in different directions. When he reported this strange sight, Bernard discovered that two policemen and an army engineer had seen it too.

In December 1978, an Australian TV crew filmed a blazing light which experts concluded 'may be a spaceship'. In early 1979, 'an illuminated ping-pong ball, rotating, pulsating and darting around' was filmed over South Island, New Zealand.

THE EVIDENCE

A boomerang-shaped UFO was seen by over a hundred witnesses in Arizona, USA in 1981. It swooped down on a copper-smelting plant, silently hovered then sped off.

In 1994, a Swedish woman driving home saw a bright, rectangular light with jagged spikes. Her car engine instantly cut out. She ran for help but when she returned the light had disappeared and the car started normally.

In Argentina in 1995, a Boeing 734 was coming in to land when the airport lost power and was plunged into darkness. The plane aborted its landing and was climbing upwards when the crew apparently noticed a pulsating orange and green dish hovering close by which then escorted them back to the airport. This extraordinary event was also witnessed by a military aircraft which was in the vicinity.

Throughout 1996, worldwide reports flooded in of triangular objects hovering in the sky before accelerating off at great speed. An aircraft crew claimed to have almost collided with one over Derbyshire, Britain.

THE THEORIES

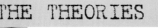

Planets and stars Jupiter, Venus and bright stars are often mistaken for UFOs as are meteors or satellites falling to Earth.

Natural phenomena Gas, birds, light reflecting off cloud, light-show lasers or cloud shapes may explain sightings.

Earth lights Strange lights that change shape may appear above fault lines in the Earth where a strong electrical field is present, particularly before, during or after earthquakes.

Optical illusion The way light reflects through the atmosphere might cause mirage-like images to appear in the sky.

Wish fulfilment When physicist David Simpson secretly flew a kite, balloon and lighted torch-bulb in front of a group of UFO watchers, some described what they saw as 'brighter than any man-made light', flashing a code and even communicating telepathically.

Aircraft At night aircraft lights are easily mistaken for UFOs. In daylight an aircraft can reflect the sun so brightly it cannot clearly be seen.

Military technology Top-secret technology means that aircraft could be far more advanced than we know. Witnesses may mistake the latest military test-plane for a UFO.

WHAT SCIENCE SAYS

Scientists and researchers have come up with a new term for many sightings: Unidentified Atmospheric Phenomenon (UAP). It is used to describe UFO sightings for which there is no obvious explanation, but which researchers believe probably relate to natural causes. This term is important because it shifts the focus away from aliens in outer space. In general, UFO-logists think that just 1% of all sightings relate to a kind of flying vehicle!

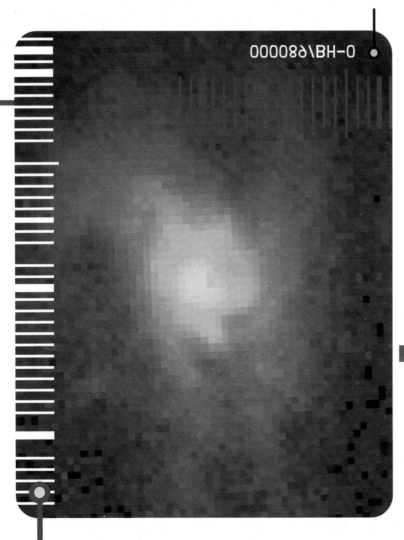

000080\BH-0

What Do You Think?

Have you ever seen something in the sky that you've been unable to identify?

Would you believe your best friend if they told you they had seen a UFO?

If aliens really are out there, why are they not making more direct contact with us?

Should governments spend more money on watching the skies?

Why might aliens be interested in observing Earth?

How easy do you think it would be to fake a UFO photograph?

Will we ever be able to send spacecraft to far away galaxies?

Alien Abductions

For centuries, according to some believers, people have been taken aboard alien ships against their will (abducted). Long ago, people feared they might be whisked away by fairy folk, but nowadays the fairies seem to have been replaced by alien beings who use their victims for medical experiments.

THE MYSTERY

Thousands of people worldwide claim to have been taken by aliens. Are these just modern-day fairy tales or are some people really being kidnapped by uninvited extraterrestrial visitors?

THE EVIDENCE

American Richard Miller was abducted in the 1950s. The aliens told him they were part of a 'Universal Confederation' of more than 680 planets, whose advanced evolution gave them right of membership. Apparently Earth would remain excluded until its people achieved greater spiritual awareness.

In 1961, Americans Barney and Betty Hill were driving along a deserted road when they claim to have been abducted by a strange craft. On board, human-like creatures with ice-blue eyes carried out medical experiments on them which were not yet known in the 1960s.

In 1975,
Argentinian Carlos Diaz says he was walking home from work early one morning when he was blinded by a pulsating light that lifted him into the air. He remembered three green-skinned creatures painlessly pulling hair from his head. Four hours later, he found himself 800 km away. Doctors could not understand how his hair had been pulled out without damaging the roots.

While on patrol in 1979, Scottish forestry worker Bob Taylor claims he saw a grey sphere hovering just above the ground. Suddenly, what appeared to be two spiked metal balls bounced out of the object towards him. Bob remembers an overpowering, unpleasant smell and a tugging sensation at his legs before collapsing unconscious. Later, the police discovered 40 shallow holes, which could have been made by spikes, and bulldozer-like tracks. The tracks were in one small area only – as if a vehicle had come straight down from above.

One night in 1977, on a mountain in Chile, soldiers saw strange purple lights descending nearby. The lights disappeared shortly after one of them went to investigate. After fifteen minutes, he stumbled back and collapsed. Later, the others saw he had grown a beard and his watch had stopped at 4.30 am, with the date set at five days later.

THE EVIDENCE

Australian Frederick Valentich, an amateur pilot and UFO enthusiast, disappeared in 1978 while flying across the Bass Strait. His last radio conversation with air traffic controllers in Melbourne speaks of being followed by a shiny, metallic craft. Just before losing contact, Frederick said, "It is hovering and it is not an aircraft".

On 30 November 1989 in New York, Linda Napolitano alleges she was abducted from her apartment by aliens. Astonishingly, two secret-service bodyguards and a high-ranking politician watched the woman float out of her apartment and enter a UFO.

Another witness was driving over Brooklyn Bridge when the engines of the vehicles on the bridge failed. These drivers also witnessed the abduction, although no one else came forward.

UFO researcher Budd Hopkins says that the politician involved is so highly regarded that if he talked publicly about what he had seen, the whole world would believe in alien abductions!

THE THEORIES

- **Hoaxes** People claim to have been abducted because they want fame or money.

- **Dreams** Most abduction stories contain a lot of dreamlike images such as floating or moving instantly from place to place. They are more likely to be dreams than reality.

- **Aliens in trouble** Humans have something that aliens need, so people are continually kidnapped.

- **Hypnotic suggestion** Most abduction stories are uncovered under hypnosis, during which images may be triggered in the semi-conscious mind of a person, conjuring up unreal events.

- **Unity** Abduction stories are encouraged by governments in order to unite the world against an imaginary enemy.

WHAT SCIENCE SAYS

Canadian scientist Dr. Michael Persinger believes that some naturally occurring bright lights can trigger hallucinations. Because of the current popularity of alien abduction stories, a person's imagination may interpret the light as an encounter with aliens.

Alien ships always seem to be described as just slightly more advanced than our own current technological development. In the 1950s, for example, abductees described control panels with heavy levers and number counters. Today, peoples' memories are of control panels with liquid crystal displays. This again suggests that abductions are actually figments of the imagination.

What Do You Think?

Would you like to go on board an alien craft?

What questions would you ask an alien?

Why is it so difficult for people to remember their abduction experiences?

If aliens don't exist, why would so many people worldwide lie about their experiences?

Is believing in aliens a way of coping with the idea that we are the only life form in the universe?

Should we stop thinking about aliens and get on with sorting out our own planet?

Crashes and Landings

In 1949, Professor of Astronomy George Valley, a member of the Air Force Scientific Advisory Board in America, warned high-ranking officials to expect extraterrestrial visitors. He believed that US advances in rocket development and atomic power would attract inquisitive aliens.

 ## THE MYSTERY

As the whole world watches for 'flying saucers', stories of UFO crashes and landings have become increasingly common. But are these stories simply modern-day myths or are we really being visited by aliens from outer space?

THE EVIDENCE

The most famous alleged alien crash happened in July 1947 in the desert outside Roswell, New Mexico, close to a nuclear-armed US military airbase.

After a fierce storm, rancher William Brazel noticed a deep rut in the ground and a scattered trail of strange metal fragments. He took the pieces to the Sheriff's office in Roswell.

The site was cordoned off as further samples were collected and taken to the airbase. The first press releases claimed they had been 'fortunate enough to gain possession' of a 'flying disk'. Later, they said that it was just a downed weather balloon. Brazel was instructed not to talk about what he had seen and the case was closed.

Rumours about what really happened persist to this day and UFO researchers have tracked down eye witnesses. Major Marcel, the first intelligence officer on the scene commented on the material recovered from the site, stating that in his opinion it was definitely not of earthly origin.

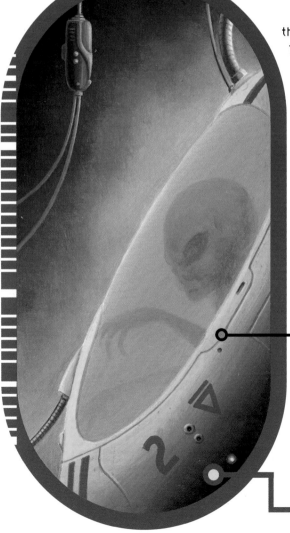

Attempts to burn the metal with a powerful blow-torch failed: although it warmed up, seconds later it was cold to the touch again.

Unearthly material was not the only thing found at the site. Civil engineer Grady Barnett stated that he came across humanoid (human-like) bodies with large domed heads.

Many were badly burned, but it is alleged that some were still alive as they were taken to the top-secret airbase. Some claim they are still held there – kept frozen in a chemical fluid!

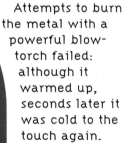

UFO CRASH SITE
1947

FOR APPT.
TO VIEW
SITE CALL
623-4043

THE EVIDENCE

In 1957, fishermen at Ubatuba Beach in Brazil stated they had seen a flying saucer explode and crash into the sea. Tests on the floating debris found that it was ultra-pure magnesium metal, produced by a method then unknown.

In August 1970, a maid at a Spanish farmhouse claims she saw a craft the size of a small car land close to a field. A humanoid being of normal height was seen studying the alfalfa crops. Next day, glowing boot prints were found on the road.

When a glowing metallic object landed in Fort Beaufort, South Africa, in 1972, police opened fire – but the bullets simply ricocheted off the craft which took off again with a humming noise.

In Wales in 1975, a teenage boy claims he saw a dome-shaped object fading in and out of sight on a hilltop. Two jelly-like beings ventured out, but quickly returned to their craft. The object then faded away.

In December 1980, two American airmen stationed in Britain spotted multi-coloured lights in Rendlesham Forest and called for back up. When military police sergeant Jim Penniston arrived, the three men clearly saw a triangular smooth-sided craft with a surface of smoky glass. It was about the size of a tank but stood on a tripod and had an inscription etched into the side. The men had difficulty walking towards the craft as if they were up against an invisible force field. The object then rose up and sped away, according to Sergeant Penniston: "faster than any aircraft I have observed".

The following day, more lights were seen by those investigating the incident.

For the past thirty years, it is claimed that peace-loving alien visitors have been welcomed by the residents of Childs, Arizona. Scientists analysed strands of silvery 'angel hair' and a strange powdery substance left after the visits but were unable to identify them.

In 1951, a farmer in Veghenza, Italy watched astounded as a white metal UFO apparently landed next to the town cemetery. After putting down metal supports and steps, six small blue-eyed creatures came out and looked around.

In 1989, in the Russian city of Voronezh, a group of children claimed to have watched a UFO shaped like a ball of fire circle around them and then settle in a tree. The aliens that emerged from inside were said to be more than three metres tall and wearing silver suits. They had dark skin, small heads and three eyes. The story was taken seriously by the Soviet authorities who had witnessed a number of UFOs around their secret air-bases for years. In all, six landings and one sighting were reported between 21 September and 28 October 1989 in this same area.

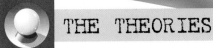

THE THEORIES

Alien missions Extraterrestrial beings are keeping an eye on Earth's technological development.

Disinformation Governments are deliberately passing on false information about UFOs to cover up what is really going on, such as the testing of top-secret weapons.

Hallucinations We cannot always believe what we see. Lack of sleep, drugs and alcohol may cause hallucinations.

Hoaxes What better way to become famous than by claiming to have seen a spacecraft land on Earth?

Scientific equipment Alien craft are rockets used to launch satellites, the satellites themselves, or meteorological (weather) equipment falling to Earth.

Secret technology Top-secret test equipment may be mistaken for alien vehicles. For example, the US air force are currently testing aircraft coatings that change colour.

Another dimension Aliens do not come from outer space but share our planet, existing in another dimension and reality close to ours.

WHAT SCIENCE SAYS

There is still no hard evidence that alien life forms have ever landed on our planet, although most astronomers will agree that some form of extraterrestrial life probably exists in the universe.

However, there is no reason to assume that these extraterrestrial life forms will resemble anything remotely human. The chances of life developing on other planets in the same way as on Earth is unlikely, which suggests that reports of alien craft landing and humanoid creatures emerging from them are even more likely to be imaginary.

What Do You Think?

If aliens have such advanced technology that they can travel light years through space, what could we have that would interest them?

If aliens are landing on our planet, why do they not do so openly?

Why would governments want to keep information about crashed alien craft secret?

How would aliens react to humans landing on their planet?

What would you do if a spacecraft landed in your garden?

Do aliens have to go through the same training as our astronauts before going into space?

If you were an alien stranded on Earth after crash-landing, how would you survive?

Hot Spots

Around the world, certain places seem to draw UFO activity, registering a far higher number of sightings than can be put down to chance alone. Such places are known as UFO 'windows' or 'hot spots'. So far, more than a hundred have been identified globally.

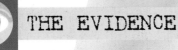

THE MYSTERY

Could extraterrestrials be homing in on certain places deliberately, or are multiple sightings imagined by frightened people?

THE EVIDENCE

After witness Kenneth Arnold spoke of seeing a craft shaped like a 'flying saucer' in June 1947, reports of 800 other sightings flooded in across America in less than a month.

Multiple sightings have occurred in Brazil and it continues to report more alien abductions than any other country. In 1980, the town of Tres Coroas was supposedly terrorised for twenty days – with balls of light chasing cars, flames appearing as if from nowhere, objects levitating and hundreds of UFO sightings.

An Arctic window opened up in the mid-1980s over the Hessdalen Valley in Norway, with blips detected on radar screens and multiple reports of strange lights in the sky.

THE THEORIES

- **Snowball effect** One sighting leads to another as people search for what they want to see.

- **Safety in numbers** People too scared to talk about an encounter now feel encouraged to do so.

Open doorways In certain places there are 'doorways' between dimensions through which beings can pass.

Military installations Some hot spots are near military bases. Airborne activity is either mistaken for, or genuinely attracts, extraterrestrial visitors.

- **Ley lines** Paths of natural energy run through the Earth and where they cross may attract alien forces.

WHAT SCIENCE SAYS

A number of researchers have found a connection between unusually large numbers of UFO reports and geological faults, or cracks in the Earth's surface (see page 10). Ideal spots for multiple UFO sightings are areas such as quarries (where the rock face is exposed) and reservoirs (where the enormous pressure of the water puts additional strain on the rock).

What Do You Think?

Would you like to live in a UFO hot spot?

Do certain places feel stranger than others?

Have you ever agreed with something just because all your friends have?

Have you ever kept quiet about something for fear of looking stupid?

If aliens target specific places, why not choose important cities such as London or Washington?

Around Britain, a UFO was filmed over Bonnybridge, Scotland in 1994; in the 1970s in Broadhaven, Wales, 15 children described a spaceship that apparently landed near their school; in 1977, numerous close encounters were reported in the Pennine Hills; and in Wiltshire, sightings were claimed of 'strange figures' over two metres tall.

Secrets and Lies

In 1976, the Spanish Air Ministry released some of its files on UFOs to reporter Juan José Benitez. After reading them, Benitez said that it was clear that, 'UFOs exist and, quite evidently, are a matter of the deepest concern to the governments of the whole planet.' But just how much do governments really know about UFOs?

THE MYSTERY

Is the truth about extraterrestrials being covered up by governments in a 'conspiracy of silence', or are stories of UFOs a shield for military, top-secret activities?

THE EVIDENCE

A top-secret American panel, codenamed 'Majestic 12', was allegedly set up in 1947 to investigate UFOs. Its existence continues to be officially denied. However, a Majestic 12 report of 1952 confirms the recovery of four alien bodies from a crash site in Roswell, New Mexico.

A number of official projects have been set up by the US government to investigate UFOs such as 'Project Blue Book' (1952–1969), but researcher William Moore believes more exist. They include Project Aquarius on alien life-forms; Project Sigma on communication with aliens; Project Pounce, listing UFOs in government possession; and Project Snowbird, which test-flies captured alien craft.

THE THEORIES

Information exchange Extraterrestrial technology is so advanced, that governments have made secret deals to swap information in return for human abductions.

Suspicion People suspect those in authority and often think they may be telling lies.

Top-secret weapons Governments are not hiding the truth about UFOs but covering up their own activities, such as testing top-secret weapons.

In Australia, UFOs are investigated by the Air Force who report no evidence of extraterrestrials. In 1953, however, film of a UFO sent for investigation was returned to its owner minus the frames showing the alien craft.

According to Albert K. Bender and other witnesses the Men in Black (MIBs) are real. Their mission is to stop UFO experiences becoming public knowledge by whatever means possible. In 1953, they visited Bender, warning him to give up his internationally known Flying Saucer Bureau.

In Texas in 1980, Betty Cash had radiation sickness after seeing a UFO followed by 23 Chinook helicopters. Believing the craft to be state property, she unsuccessfully sued the American government for her suffering. No one has ever admitted owning the Chinook helicopters.

Although French organization GEPAN officially investigates UFOs, it is claimed that certain cases are secretly investigated elsewhere.

WHAT SCIENCE SAYS

When the files of the official US Air Force UFO investigation, Project Blue Book, were released in the 1970s, they showed that little had been discovered. Astronomer J. Allen Hynek, US government adviser on Project Blue Book, did not accuse the government of a cover-up, but believed the air force were only interested in explaining away rather than investigating UFOs.

What Do You Think?

Should governments be allowed to keep certain secrets for the sake of security?

What reasons might governments have for keeping information about UFOs to themselves?

What would happen if people discovered a government had known of the existence of aliens all along?

Can we believe everything the media tells us?

Aliens from Long Ago

Reports of strange objects in the sky date back centuries. In those days, they were interpreted as fairies or fire-breathing dragons, not alien spacecraft. Today, some people believe that our world was visited by extraterrestrials thousands of years ago and that it was their superior wisdom and technology that built ancient monuments such as the Egyptian pyramids. ——o

 THE MYSTERY

Have extraterrestrials been watching us for a lot longer than we have been watching them?

THE EVIDENCE

The earliest recorded sighting was during the reign of Egyptian pharaoh Thutmose III, in about 1450 BCE. Described as a 'circle of fire in the sky' a witness also noted 'the breath of its mouth had a foul odour'.

In the 4th century AD, Julius Obsequens wrote of 'ships in the sky' seen over Italy.

In 1254, a 'kind of large ship, elegantly shaped, well-equipped and of marvellous colour' was seen in the sky over St Albans, England.

The people of Basel, Switzerland reported 'black and red globes moving at great speed' through the sky in 1566.

In 1783, a UFO was seen performing aerobatics over the River Thames Valley, England. Scientist Tiberius Cavallo described it as changing shape and colour, moving speedily with sudden changes of direction, then splitting in two and disappearing.

In 1897, American politician Alexander Hamilton issued a sworn statement that he had witnessed a cigar-shaped craft land near his Kansas farm which was, 'occupied by six of the strangest beings I ever saw'.

In 1950, archaeologists in Mexico uncovered ancient Mayan carvings of a man surrounded by levers and machinery in a capsule with a fiery tail similar to exhaust fumes.

For hundreds of years, the Dogon Tribe of Mali, West Africa have worshipped intelligent, fish-like gods from the star

Sirius – which was not discovered by modern telescopes until the 1950s. The Dogons' advanced knowledge has amazed modern scientists.

Some people believe the ancient stone statues of Easter Island were created by alien visitors, not only because of their immense size but also because the carved faces are not like those of the islanders.

THE THEORIES

- **Meteors** Many sightings of 'fire in the sky' may have been meteor showers which were not understood until the 1900s.

- **Natural phenomena** Some research matches medieval sightings with unusual geological conditions which were little understood at the time.

- **Alien aid** Superior beings from outer space have been visiting Earth for centuries, helping in our development.

Hysteria Different things trigger the imaginations of different societies. In the late 1800s, with the arrival of the first airships, hundreds of 'airship sightings' were being recorded. One Kansas farmer even accused the airships of cattle theft!

- **Hoaxes** Many accounts of strange sightings and landings were the work of journalists hoping to increase falling newspaper sales.

WHAT SCIENCE SAYS

In the nineteenth century, with the development of astronomy into a more accurate science, the quality and quantity of UFO records increased. Today, our growing knowledge of space leads scientists to the conclusion that we may not be alone in the universe.

Claims that ancient monuments and landmarks have been left for us by previous generations of visiting aliens are generally ignored by researchers. For example, in 1956, the inhabitants of Easter Island successfully carved and erected a new giant statue using only traditional methods. They did this in answer to claims of UFO enthusiasts that islanders could not have constructed the statues without alien help.

What Do You Think?

Do you think dragons once inhabited Earth, flying through the sky and breathing fire?

If aliens have been visiting us for hundreds of years, why haven't they taken over the planet by now?

If aliens had the technology for space travel centuries ago, how far has their scientific knowledge developed today?

Will the stories of UFO sightings made today seem ridiculous to people 500 years into the future?

Glossary

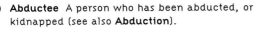

Abductee A person who has been abducted, or kidnapped (see also **Abduction**).

Alien Abduction The kidnapping of a human by **extraterrestrials**.

Aliens *see* **Extraterrestrials**.

Angel hair Fine threads, similar to a spider's web, that fall from the sky and may be an unexplained natural phenomenon.

Archaeologist A scientist who studies archaeology – the investigation of human history through examining remains found at historical sites.

Astronomer A scientist who studies astronomy – the investigation of space, the stars and planets.

Central Intelligence Agency (CIA) The US government department that collects secret information.

Close encounter Contact with **extraterrestrials** or UFOs. There are three kinds: a close encounter of the first kind is a sighting of an extraterrestrial or UFO; a close encounter of the second kind is when evidence of an encounter is left behind; a close encounter of the third kind is a meeting with, or abduction by extraterrestrials.

Conspiracy of silence An agreement to say nothing.

Dimension A state of existence, or reality. Some people believe that different realities, or worlds, may exist alongside our own.

Disinformation False information that is meant to hide the truth.

Earth lights Lights that appear in the sky above fault lines in the Earth.

Electrical field A region or area where a high level of electricity is present.

Extraterrestrial encounters *see* **Close encounters**.

Extraterrestrials Beings that are supposed to come from outer space, also called **aliens**.

Fault lines Breaks in the layers of rock that make up the Earth's surface.

Flying saucer A name for an unidentified flying object (UFO), introduced in 1947 when American Kenneth Arnold witnessed flying discs that moved like 'skipping saucers'.

Galaxy A star system such as our own galaxy or Milky Way. There are many separate galaxies in space.

Geological conditions The arrangement of the rock layers that make up the Earth.

Geological fault see Fault lines.

Hallucination A vision or experience conjured up by a person's mind that seems quite real.

Humanoid A word to describe an animal or a thing that looks like a human.

Hypnosis The trance-like 'sleep' that is caused by the words or actions of a hypnotist.

Identified Flying Object (IFO) The name by which a strange object reported to have been in the sky is classified, once an explanation for it is found.

Intelligence officer A person employed by an intelligence agency, such as the CIA, whose job is to collect secret information of military or political importance.

Ley lines Invisible straight lines that criss-cross the Earth connecting certain ancient sites, thought by some to be paths of natural energy.

Light years In astronomy, one light year is equal to the distance light travels in a year – about 9.6 million million kilometres.

Men in Black (MiBs) In the 1950s and 60s, some UFO researchers were visited by men dressed in identical black suits who advised them to abandon their investigations. Some believed the men to be government agents, others that they were **extraterrestrials**.

Meteor A collection of matter from outer space, such as rock and metal, that travels at great speed through space and is seen from Earth as a moving streak of light.

Military technology Weapons, military craft and other equipment that are often developed secretly.

Natural phenomenon (plural: phenomena) Something produced by nature (such as an earthlight) that is not fully understood by science.

Physicist A scientist who studies physics – the investigation of the minute particles which make up everything in the known universe.

Radiation sickness Illness caused by exposure to dangerous radioactive waves, such as X-rays.

St. Elmo's Fire The name given to a brightly shining light often seen during a storm and caused by a powerful discharge of static electricity.

Static electricity Electricity that does not flow in a continuous current but forms into a ball or other shape.

Telepathic communication Communicating with another person through the mind.

Ufologist A person who studies UFOs and extraterrestrial life.

Unidentified Atmospheric Phenomenon (UAP) The name scientists use for UFO sightings which are likely to be due to natural causes.

Unidentified Flying Object (UFO) A mysterious, unknown object seen in the sky, thought to be an alien space craft.

Universe All forms of matter and energy that exist and the space in which they exist.

Index